Revolution *Is* a Dinner Party

–Rogue Pluralism in China

by M. Eigh

ISBN-13: 978-1484821893

ISBN-10: 1484821890

eISBN: 978-0-9891776-0-3

~~~

Send comments or questions to:

Eigh.com@gmail.com

~~~

"Witty and irreverent, as well as scholarly and insightful, M. Eigh's new book Revolution is a Dinner Party offers readers a rare insider's view of China's shifting political and cultural climate"

-- Tina Walton

"Worthwhile Peek inside Chinese Culture."

-- Lynda Belcher

"...Educational yet Entertaining...I would recommend it to anyone that is interested in current Chinese politics, society, and culture."

-- Fabiola Gutierrez

~~~

If you liked this book, please post your review on Amazon, or send it to me.

Hearty thanks – M. Eigh

Eigh.com@gmail.com

~~~

Table of Contents

Prologue

Mao Zedong, founding dictator of Communist China and one of the 20th century's most provocative philosophers, said, "A revolution is not a dinner party, or writing an essay, or painting a picture, or doing embroidery; it cannot be so refined, so leisurely and gentle, so temperate, kind, courteous, restrained and magnanimous. A revolution is an insurrection, an act of violence by which one class overthrows another." [i]

Mao's words ring true, when considered in the context of 20th century China. Virtually no social and economic progress was ever introduced without a revolution; and no revolution was ever successful without violence. So much so that Mao concluded, "Political power grows out of the barrel of a gun." [ii]

Mao's wisdom, reflected in these uncompromising assertions, was proved true again and again in the Cold War era's brutal politics. Marxists and Socialist practitioners who dared to deviate from Mao's doctrine have inflicted demise on their causes and, in some cases, their own lives. Such fatalism was dramatically exemplified in the 1973 Chilean coup d'état that toppled the democratically elected, albeit communist, President Salvador Allende.

Allende believed that socialism could be achieved via parliamentary victory. When besieged by troops loyal to the CIA-backed usurper[iii], Army Commander-in-Chief Augusto Pinochet, he purportedly took his own life with an AK-47 after delivering a swansong speech on live radio. The rifle was a gift from Fidel Castro and bore a gold plate engraved: "To my good friend Salvador from Fidel, who by different means tries to achieve the same goals."[iv]

It is only natural that generations of Chinese who grew up in Mao's China have taken it for granted that military power equals political power, and social progress entails revolution, hence inevitably violence.

Revolution is not a dinner party: Mao's Red Guards manhandling Marshall Peng Dehuai who alienated Mao, circa 1967.

Although Gorbachev-style glasnost and perestroika did not fare well in China and the 1989 Tiananmen Square mass student protest was met with a massacre – hence proving Mao's wisdom once again – the largely bloodshed-free collapse of the Soviet Union eventually shattered that deeply imbued belief.

Today, the majority of average Chinese believe that the Chinese government has to and will redress the 1989 Tiananmen Square Massacre. More importantly, they do not imply that such a fundamental shift in the government's political stance can only be obtained in a violent revolution that overthrows the ruling Communist Party of China. Rather, they believe that it is just a matter of time before the Party itself will instigate the shift. There are signs that the breaking of the 1989 Tiananmen Square Massacre taboo may have already begun. On Jan. 17, 2013, an officially approved translation of Ezra Vogel's Lionel Gelber Prize winner, *Deng Xiaoping and the Transformation of China*, was released in mainland China by SDX Joint Publishing Company. Remarkably, the translation has retained roughly three quarters of the book's original text on the 1989 Tiananmen Square Incident.[v]

What is causing the average Chinese to dismiss Mao's teachings that they used to regard as immortal truth?

The answer, the author believes, depends on the angle of analysis. But some indisputable facts have been, without a doubt, contributory. First off, two-thirds of China's 1.34 billion people are under the age of 35,[vi] which means two-thirds of today's Chinese were born after Mao's death and have been spared the brainwash that was the staple of the Mao era. Secondly, the fabric and culture of Chinese society has undergone a sea change since Mao's passing.

This book does not aim to provide that general answer. Rather, it strives to bring your attention to the new phenomena in today's China that make it such a dynamic, evolving nation. These phenomena are anecdotal evidence that the most crass and rudimentary forms of democracy may be penetrating the Chinese society at its grass-root level.

In other words, this book presents a China that sharply contrasts with the subsistent yet utopian China depicted by Michelangelo Antonioni in his renowned 1972 documentary *Chung Kuo, China.* As was demonstrated in the infantile stage of two most recent democracies, Republic of Korea (South Korea) and Republic of China (Taiwan), a burgeoning democracy first has to test its constituents' collective willingness to tolerate pluralism. (Remember the TV clips of Parliament brawls in those countries?) Like a petri dish, a burgeoning democracy gives birth to things not only good and beautiful, but also evil and ugly.

And even what is good, evil, beautiful and ugly are up for debate in today's China. Unanimity has died. It cannot even feign an existence in a symbolic vote in the National People's Congress, China's rubberstamp parliament. There are always a few *enfants terribles* who ruin a perfect unanimous vote by opposing or abstaining.

That is the viral power of burgeoning pluralism this book tries to depict. Since there are many ugly and ridiculous elements in the expanding universe of such pluralism, the author has decided to refer to it as rogue pluralism.

This unflattering term, coined by the author, reflects the bacterial vitality of any new trends and fads in the world's most populous nation. Despite being the second largest economy in the world, China, burdened by the world's largest population, ranks number 90 in per capita GDP, with a measly $5,417, as opposed to the U.S., which ranks number 14 with a per capita GDP of $48,328.[vii] Therefore, this term also reflects the hardscrabble nature of pluralism in China.

Often unattractive notwithstanding, rogue pluralism may be the pivotal and seminal first trimester of a democratic China. Through this humble book, the author hopes that its Western readers will cherish and celebrate China's rogue pluralism as much as the Chinese.

Pluralism begets tolerance. Tolerance begets democracy. The answer for a better China does not lie in regime change, as has happened in its history, from the numerous incarnations of feudal dynasties, to post-monarch chaos in 20th century. If the totalitarian communist government were to be overthrown and replaced with new party driven by a new utopian ideology, history would merely repeat, with millions of lives sacrificed for the sake of feel-good, yet furtive cause, as has happened so many times before.

Fortunately, rogue pluralism is on the rise in China. It has hence become less likely that a bloody revolution to overthrow the communist regime will befall the world's most populous nation. With virtually every citizen a stakeholder in a more tolerant society, today's majority of Chinese are more interested in establishing a fair and just process that enables them to coexist peacefully in their unprecedented march to prosperity.

Age of Innocence, **Acrylic on canvas by the author. ©All rights reserved.**

Farces vs. Gravitas

The legendary Chinese filmmaker, Mr. Feng Xiaogang, released his epic big-budget production *Back to 1942* ("一九四二") on November 29, 2012 in mainland Chinese theaters. *Back to 1942* took Feng 17 years and three attempts to complete, and featured Oscar winners Adrien Brody and Tim Robbins.

It grossed approximately ¥20 million on its opening day, a number that pales in comparison to the opening sales of Feng's previous films. In 2011, *Aftershock* (唐山大地震) grossed ¥36 million and in 2010, *If You Are the One 2* (非诚勿扰 2) raked in ¥33 million.

In the meantime, *Lost in Thailand* (人在囧途之泰囧), a low-budget, *Hangover*-esque road film released in December 2012, had already broken five box office records in China by the mid-December — including those for best opening day and highest single-day income for a domestic movie. After just eight days of release, the flick had earned about ¥450 million — or $72.2 million. *Lost in Thailand* went on to be the highest-grossed domestic film ever produced in China, breaking the record of ¥1 billion by the end of 2012.

Back to 1942 is Feng's bold and daring inquisition into the historic composition of the great famine that befell China's Henan province in the winter of 1942. It killed more than 3 million people, a tragedy compounded by the Japanese invasion. *Lost in Thailand,* on the other hand, is a light-hearted assembly of slapstick loosely strung together with some forgettable plots.

While Feng himself purportedly was bitter about Chinese audiences' general apathy towards his epic, enthusiastic theater-goers celebrated *Lost in Thailand* rather shamelessly. They find Feng's attempt to find answers to a historical tragedy "preachy." Numerous blog, forum and comment posts claim that *Lost in Thailand* epitomizes the kind of "entertainment" the Chinese people enjoy and deserve.

The Chinese word for entertainment consists of two characters: "娱" (yú, meaning "amusement") and "乐" (lè, meaning "joy"). Since Chinese is a language populated and plagued with countless homophonic characters (Chinese: 同音字/tóng yīn zì: characters that are pronounced the same way but may differ in meanings), these posters have playfully, and rather poignantly, substituted the first character with an easy homophonic replacement, "愚" (yú, meaning "silly", "stupid"). Hence, these Chinese audiences have shunned the self-righteous literati's by calling entertainment "愚乐" (silly fun) instead of "娱乐". (entertainment)

Perhaps, in "silly fun," many Chinese find a sanctuary from the standard fare of communist brainwashers. Cheap comedies like *Lost in Thailand* blatantly pander to their hostility toward anything preachy. As younger generations of Chinese become more and more assertive in their life styles, farce tends to fare better than gravitas in China's vast entertainment market. After all, if all things entertaining were required to possess a heavy dose of "educational" value under Mao's rule, today, anything farcical is all but void of educational value and hence refreshing, and anything meant to be thought-provoking can be found guilty of mind manipulation.

Vulgarianism vs. Censorship

China's traditional two-man standup stage comedy "Xiangsheng (相声)", better known in the West as Crosstalk, has enjoyed an extraordinary boom in recent decades. Many Xiangsheng comedians have certifiably become China's *nouveau riche*. Among them, Mr. Guo Degang (郭德纲), a Tianjin native, purportedly takes in an annual ¥15 million. His Taiwanese counterparts can hardly hide their jealousy when talking about how much better the mainland Xiangsheng market is. While Xiangsheng millionaires in mainland China can afford luxury cars and villas, their Taiwanese counterparts often make fun of their own small high-rise apartments and their 1.3L engine cars.

The script of a Xiangsheng act, with its clever puns and allusions, is impossible to translate and hard for a non-Chinese speaker to appreciate. But if I am to describe where China's Xiangsheng is going, I would say it is going to "grossland." Comedians are pulling no punches and stopping at nothing to earn a giggle.

The language can be foul, the subject matter gross, and the spirit mean. But it can also be hellishly funny. It tickles your fancy, or your vice, if you really have to analyze it. There is an element of abandon in the way the Xiangsheng comedians try to gross you out, expose your character fault, or demonstrate street-smartness. Megan Stack had this to say in the Los Angeles Times about Guo Degang:

> *"He's foulmouthed. He's subversive. He has no respect for authority. In a country where an insurgent spirit can land you behind bars, it made Guo Degang rich instead. Sometimes he stands onstage and gripes like a curmudgeon who's plopped down next to you on a bus. In his own theaters and on the road, he talks about his life, his struggles, mundane things. But it comes with intricate wordplays,*

adroit use of slang, unexpected bursts of rhyme that resist translation into English. "[viii]

In 2006, then-General Party Secretary Hu Jintao launched a propaganda campaign against what he characterized as the "three vulgarities:" sex-obsessed, mindless and tasteless culture. For a while, Guo's books were yanked from bookstore shelves, his theatres had their licenses revoked and his performances were canceled left and right. In the following years, the government and state-run media made many attempts to defame him. Among the most notable were the so-called "Villagate" and the "Apprentice Assaultgate." The first referred to a report by Beijing TV that alleged that Guo's Beijing villa encroached onto "public green land." The second referred to an altercation between the paparazzi and one of Guo's apprentices in the investigation of the "Villagate."

In defiance, Guo stood up and openly mocked of the anti-vulgarity campaign. To the chagrin of China's ruling elite, Guo's flagrant disobedience gained him even more popularity. His attitude resembled that of Ah Q, the hero in *the True Story of Ah Q*,[ix] by Lu Xun, who was arguably China's most influential author in the 20th century. In one famous scene, Ah Q came across with a nun on the street and molested her. His rationale was, "If the monks can touch her, why can't I?" Such deep-rooted distrust of the Chinese public toward those who self-aggrandize their own moral footing had yet another incarnation in Guo's public defiance: "Yes, it is vulgar, but so what? I like it. We like it."

What was almost but not quite said, was: "So what? I'm sure you hypocrites also like it. You just wouldn't ever admit it. And if the monks can do it, why can't I?"

In Lu Xun's story, tragedy befell Ah Q after his reckless and defiant action. He was beat up by street gangs. Guo Degang, however, survived the bully of the formidable state media and propaganda campaign. He still performs on stage, proffering jokes while raking in a fortune, all at the expense of the totalitarian government's censorship.

If Guo Degang was the trailblazer, his emboldening example has been well followed. On April 30, 2012, a pair of Xiangsheng actors, Jia Xuming (贾旭明) and Zhang Kang (张康) set a new record in pushing the limit of Chinese state censorship: they performed a hilarious mock episode of CCTV (China Central TV) News.

The 7 o'clock prime time news broadcast is Communist China's most sacred propaganda routine. Its two-anchor format and lead-in music has not changed since the 1980's. The idea that someone dared fake an episode of CCTV News already brought out chuckles, if only tentative. But the pair pulled no punches. Their mockery of China's social ills was direct and precise, and downright merciless. In one of the funniest moments of their act, Jia Xuming announced that the aging elite communist cadres had decided to get together and re-enact their historical Long March when the Red Army was hunted by the Nationalist Army back in the early 1930's. Nine out of ten Red Army men were killed during the Long March but a total of about 9,000 of them survived, a proud victory forever enshrined in Chinese Communist textbooks and depicted in Edgar Snow's *Red Star over China.*

Zhang Kang, in a move typical of CCTV News anchors, expanded on Jia Xuming's bogus announcement. But what he said shocked the nation for a brief moment, before they found themselves laughing their hearts out. He told the audience that the aging cadres' dying wish had generated overwhelming response from the entire country. "Everybody, man or women, old or young, has volunteered to join the Nationalist Army."

Ouch. If the laugh is any indication, there is not much love or respect for the Chinese Communist Party. If the dead Red Army soldiers could hear their countrymen's laugh at their misfortune, they would know that they had died in vein.

***Cheered in China*, Poster by the author.**
©All rights reserved.

Pidginization vs. Purism

Like Latin, the Chinese language is an organism unto its own. It has a natural defense against foreign influence. For argument's sake, I am ignoring the phonetic complexities that break the spoken Chinese language down into numerous dialects. My discussion of pidginization of the Chinese language in recent decades focuses on the written language. Since the *lingua franca* of China is Mandarin, when a pronunciation is cited for a pidginized word, its Mandarin pronunciation is used.

The Chinese language has a congenital self-defense mechanism and has remained a puristic language for the large part in a modern world where cultural and linguistic barriers are becoming less and less prohibitive. Chinese is probably the only language in the world that naturally resists phonetic importation of foreign vocabulary.

There are two reasons that can explain the xenophobia of the Chinese language. One, Chinese is written in characters, a pictographic system that allows infinite remix of components of character, called *radicals*, to create new characters for representation of new concepts. This gives Chinese leeway to create vocabulary *ad hoc* to match a foreign word. Two, unlike Japanese, which has a dedicated set of alphabets (katagana) to represent all imported words, the Chinese language relies on characters solely. To phonetically import a foreign word is hence laborious and also very hard to standardize. The phonetic approximation of a foreign word can be represented with many different sets of characters, due to the large population of homophones in Chinese language.

Historically, the small population of phonetically imported foreign words have all taken a long time to standardize. For example, 阿斯

匹林 (aspirin) and 蒙太奇 (montage) have been standardized after a long period of circulation, and their character composition are now indisputable. Up till about twenty years ago, settling on a set of Chinese characters to represent a phonetically imported foreign word has always required consensus and time.

That boat has sailed. Today, the Chinese language is littered with casually imported – and mainly English – foreign words. Words are being phonetically imported not because the Chinese language lacks their counterpart vocabularies, but because they fit better with the modern ethos. The Chinese mass quickly adapts to these words due to many different, case-by-case reasons. But the main reason is these words provide a sense of connection to the world and they also circumvent certain clumsiness of their native Chinese language counterparts.

粉丝 (Fěnsī), for example, is a whimsical phonetic approximation in Chinese for the English word "fans." To the old fashioned or oblivious, this word may still mean "vermicelli." But for the majority of Chinese who are Web-savvy and have kept up with the times, it undoubtedly means "fans." If you copy and paste 粉丝 into Google Translate, the English translation will be a definitive "fans." Google does not even entertain the alternate meaning any longer.

Similar examples abound. 秀 (xiù), originallly meaning "beautiful", sounds like the English word "show" and is now used to refer to "show". To do a show is 作(zuò, "to do")秀(xiù, "show"). Reality show in Chinese is therefore 真人(zhēnrén, real person)秀(xiù, "show").

When phonetic approximation fails or falls short of perfection, the Chinese resort to literal translation for vocabulary import. For example, try to simulate the pronunciation of "catwalk" with a bunch of Chinese characters and you will find all your permutations difficult to memorize and the combination of the characters meaningless. Thus the introduction of 猫步(māobù, cat step).

Similarly, "flashers" is translated as 闪族(shǎn zú, flashing cult).

Bullied and ravaged by Western industrial powers, the Chinese suffered incorrigible xenophobia in the last centuries. The knee-jerk protectionism in their language was a mere reflection of their overall distrust on all things Western. Today, the influx of randomly imported or Western-inspired words has invaded every corner of Chinese life. Some of this "unofficial" vernacular have made their way into the Communist mouthpieces such as *the People's Daily*, by accident if not by design. It is just a matter of time before these words with foreign blood acquire permanent residency in the Chinese language.

As the great Greek Stoic philosopher Epictetus said some 2,000 years ago, people are disturbed not by things but by the views they take of them. Same goes for the flip side. The Chinese are embracing loan words in their language because the concepts reflected in those vocabularies are no longer off-limits to them, no longer alien to them, and no longer threatening to them.

Cyber Slang vs. *People's Daily*

There is one other thing about the movie *Lost in Thailand* that makes it stand out. Its title in Chinese, "人在囧途之泰囧", contains an ancient Chinese character, "囧". It is a rarely or never used character and means "brightness" originally. However, it has come to mean "cornered", "frustrated" or "embarrassed" on the Web. The filmmakers pandered to this fad and embraced it in the film's title.

囧(jiǒng, frustrating, embarrassing) is just one of newly-minted words of China's rapidly growing cyber slang They are the product of clever character play and demonstrate the trivialization of conventional ideology.

Occupy a character. The first type of cyber slang words are ancient characters that went out of circulation long time ago. 囧 (jiǒng, frustrating, embarrassing) is a perfect example. As is typical of this group, its meaning is strictly "inferred" from the pictorial characteristics. In this particular case of 囧, the character is interpreted as a person held hostage in a confining space.

Smart-aleck homophones. The second type of cyber slang words are disrespectful pranks on Chinese words and phrases that bear serious meanings. A word in this group is pronounced exactly as its conventional counterpart, and is supposed to mean the same thing; however, since its characters have been replaced with homophones, they have acquired a satirical secondary meaning. For example, the Chinese word for tragedy is 悲剧(bēijù), but often when it is used on the Web, it is replaced with 杯具(bēijù) – theater props. Since corruption is rampant in China and even the elites of academia are not immune, the word for professors, 教授 (jiào shòu), has been replaced on the Web by 叫兽 (jiào shòu), or "howling beasts".

One of top ten most used words in 2012 was the Chinese word for Alexander. It comes with four characters: 亚历山大 (yàlìshāndà). The four character combination does not provide a meaning. They are there purely for the purpose of phonetic approximation. However, if one is to substitute the first two characters 亚历 (yàlì) with 压力 (yàlì, "pressure"), the Chinese word for Alexander becomes 压力山大(same pronunciation: yàlìshāndà) and it instantly acquires an alternate meaning – *pressure/distress is as heavy as a mountain*. (压力: pressure or distress; 山大: as large/heavy as a mountain.)

Eureka! The third type of cyber slang words are ingenious creations that past generations of Chinese could never even dream of. Like acronyms in English, these newly conjured words have a great deal of economy. They are concise and precise. Often, they paint a vivid picture of various social malaises.

One remarkable example of this group is 躺枪 (tǎng qiāng). Literally translated into English, the word means "lying gun," and does not make any sense. The same puzzlement is shared by Chinese who have never heard the word before. But those who have used it know that it refers to a situation bad enough to turn innocent bystanders into collateral damage. A situation so bad that you get shot even if you dive to and stay down on the ground.

Another outstanding example of this group is 屌丝 (diǎosī). 屌 (diǎo) is an vulgar word referring to penis. 丝 (sī) is the second character in the phonetically imported word "fans". It is hard to find a precise equivalent for it in English but the rough translation would be "dick faces." It refers to the bitterly disenfranchised young Chinese males who often describe themselves as short, ugly, poor, clumsy and unpolished. Sociology experts have equated a typical 屌丝 with Lu Xun's Ah Q, the only difference being that a 屌丝 (diǎosī) is much more self-conscious about his social dilemmas.

The word 屌丝 (diǎosī) made history on Nov. 3, 2012 when *People's Daily* used it in a special report about the ongoing Eighteenth Party Congress. The report cited 屌丝心态 (roughly, dick face/loser attitude) as one of the knee-jerk reactions to the impact of China's market economy. Nobody really cared what the *People's Daily* said about the 屌丝 culture, but its glorious debut in the Party's mouthpiece signified the rude awakening of China's ruling elites. After all, the cyber slang has become a formidable social phenomenon they have to deal with. And they have chosen – to their credit – to not go into denial, but to acknowledge its popularity.

The ugly Chinese. The fourth and last group of the Cyber slangs are self-effacing catchphrases. They can be an existing word or phrase that has acquired a new meaning, or a newly coined phrase that has seen overwhelming circulation. For example, the phrase 中国式

(zhōngguó shì) has a generic meaning: Chinese style; however, it is nowadays used to refer to things you see happening "only in China." When someone talks about a Chinese-style pedestrian crossing, for example, they are reminding you that anywhere in China, pedestrians pay no attention to the traffic lights and start crossing the road when they think there are "plenty" of them.

Another good example is 我爸是李刚 (My Dad is Li Gang.)[x] The phrase was first uttered by an infamous drunken driver, the 22-year-old Li Qiming (李启铭). On the evening of October 16, 2010, his black Volkswagen Magotan hit two university students on the campus of Hebei University in Baoding in Hebei province. One of the victims, 20-year-old Chen Xiaofeng (陈晓凤), died later in the hospital. The other victim, Zhang Jingjing, aged 19, remained in a stable condition, albeit suffering from a fractured left leg. Li tried to escape the scene and continued driving to the female dormitory to drop off his girlfriend. When confronted by security guards, Li was eager to reveal that that his father, Li Gang (李刚), was the deputy director of the local public security bureau. Convinced his father's position would give him immunity, he shouted out: "Go ahead, report me if you dare. My dad is Li Gang!"

Overnight, after eyewitness reports and photos of the incident went viral online, the phrase caught on fire with the Chinese. Nothing could have revealed better the inflated sense of privilege of those in power in China. Nothing could have made a better mockery of laws in China that could be trampled by those in power. If you witness an outrageous injustice committed by those in power in China, say "My father is Li Gang."

License to Kill. **Digital art by the author. ©All rights reserved.**

In 2012, the Chinese word for *maternal uncle*, 表叔 (biǎo shū), took on a new meaning. The first character in the word, 表 (biǎo) means *maternal* in its original context. And the second character 叔 (shū) means *uncle*. However, the first character can also mean *wrist watch*. After a notorious scandal surrounding a Shaanxi Province bureaucrat, this word came to refer to corrupt Chinese officials who wear brand name luxury watches. With their official salaries, any one of those watches would have taken them several lifetimes' worth of savings to purchase.

The central figure in the scandal, Mr. Yang Dacai (杨达才), chief of Shaanxi's Safety Supervision Bureau, was caught on camera grinning at the site of a horrific traffic accident that claimed 37 lives.[xi] That stupid grin on his fat face caused an outrage among the online community. A mass campaign to dig up dirt by bloggers and hackers ensued and uncovered numerous photos of this instant public enemy. With a little zooming, bloggers noticed that this man was quite a chameleon when it came to wrist watches: he wore different brands of expensive time pieces on public occasions. Purportedly, some of those watches cost in the neighborhood of $30,000.

In a country Transparency International (TI) considers as corrupt as Burkina Faso, El Salvador, Jamaica, Panama, and Peru, and more corrupt than Sri Lanka,[xii] Mr. Yang is in no lack of company. Since the incident, though, Chinese officials have been camera shy when wearing wrist watches. After all, it is impossible to rehabilitate one's reputation once labeled as a 表叔 (biǎo shū), or, a *Watch Uncle*.

On March 7, 2013, a photo of Mr. Yu Zhengsheng, the 4th-ranked member of the Chinese Communist Party's Politburo Standing Committee surfaced on Chinese social community site http://kds.pchome.net/. The photo was uploaded by a member under the username of "Brave Cruller" and shows Mr. Yu wearing a Patek Philippe that allegedly is worth €288K. The photo immediately became viral and earned Mr. Yu a new title: 表帝 (biǎo dì), or, *the Emperor of Watch Uncles*.

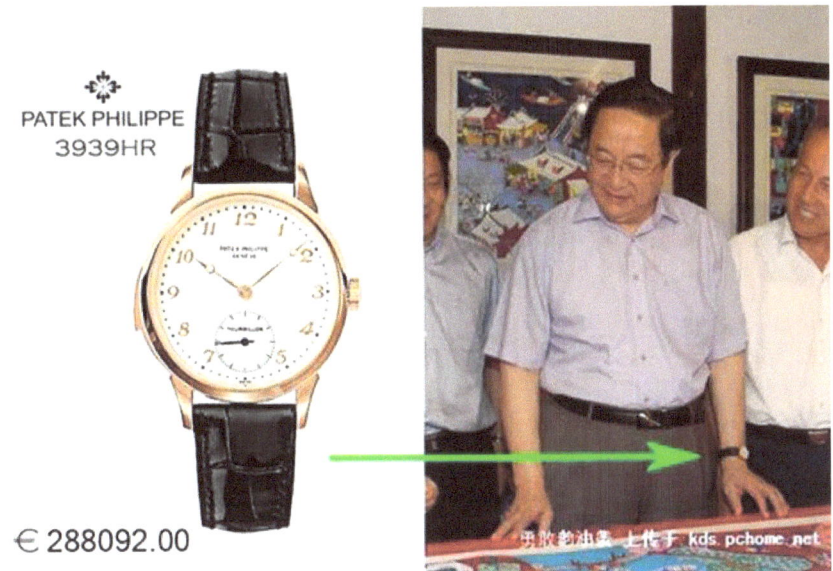

PATEK PHILIPPE
3939HR

€ 288092.00

The photo uploaded by Brave Cruller on kds.pchome.net that shows the newly minted "Emperor of All Watch Uncles", Mr. Yu Zhengsheng with a über-pricey Patek Philippe on his wrist. Source: viral. Authenticity: unverifiable.

Lei Ren vs. Lei Feng

Since 2008, the phrase lei ren (雷人,léi rén), literally, "awe-striking," has been all the rage on the Chinese Web. "When a dog bites a man, that is not news, because it happens so often. But if a man bites a dog, that is news."[xiii] That man-bites-a-dog moment can be described perfectly, in the Chinese parlance of our time, as "lei ren".

Lei Feng (雷锋, léi fēng), on the other hand, is the name of a model *People's Liberation Army* soldier who was posthumously idolized by the Chinese Communist Party's propaganda apparatus as a role model for every Chinese citizen.[xiv] In Mao's China, Lei Feng was universally worshipped and enjoyed a comparable stature to that of Jesus Christ in the Christian world.

Learn from Comrade Lei Feng, **a Cultural Revolution era propaganda poster**

Lei Feng was perfect judging by both traditional Chinese moral standards and the Chinese Communist doctrines. He was altruistic and an all-around conformist. He followed every commandments in the communist rule books and did not stand out in any aspect except for his foolhardy loyalty to the communist regime.

Mao's communist China expected its citizens to behave like Lei Feng by following two fundamental rules: The first was to stay out of trouble; the second, to do good deeds to others. In a democratic society ruled by the law, such as the U.S., whatever is not explicitly forbidden is allowed. In a totalitarian society where rulers always overwrite the rule of law, such as China, whatever is not explicitly allowed is forbidden, even if there is no specific legislation prohibiting it.

Therefore, it takes much more than just observing the law to stay out of the trouble in China. For starters, one needs to exercise vigilant self-censorship to stay out of trouble. On paper, the Chinese constitution guarantees freedom of speech. But such freedom can only be used once if you plan to speak out against the regime. Those who have chosen to do so normally end up paying for their freedom of speech in a jail cell. In the final analysis, staying out of trouble requires being a subject to the communist regime.

That has proven in recent decades to be too much to ask from the majority of today's Chinese. There have been an ever-increasing number of cases whereby a Chinese citizen has decided to take the meaning of law literally and test the hypocrisy and tolerance of the authorities. In the beginning, any who tried to test the authority got his or her fifteen minutes of fame automatically, regardless of whether their act earned them punishment or tolerance from the authorities. Gradually, it has gotten harder to earn a "lei ren" exclamation from others, as more and more people become anti-Lei

Feng and choose to assert rights that are not explicitly prohibited by the law.

The most lei ren story belongs to a certain Luo Baogen. Luo earned his world fame when the AP and Reuters news photos of his lone house standing smack in the middle of a paved Chinese highway appeared on the front pages of world media.

Luo Baogen's "Nail House" standing in the middle of the road. **Photo source: viral circulation on Chinese social networks. This is not an AP/Reuters/Getty photo**

Luo, who is in his late 60's, and his wife invested a sum in the neighborhood of ¥600K in 2001 to build their house in the town of Wenling, Zhejiang Province, only to be notified in 2008 by local authorities that they would have to relocate, as their house stand in the way of a newly planned expressway. As all neighbors accepted buyout offers or coercion from the authorities, the Luo's spurned the authorities' lowball offer of ¥210K and demanded a fair price of

¥800K. They refused to move and left the authorities no choice but to construct and pave the road around their house.

In the widely circulated AP and Reuters News photos, Luo is seen holding the title to his house lot to show he has the lawful right to stay.

Luo Baogen holding the title to his house lot. **Photo source: viral circulation on Chinese social networks. This is not an AP/Reuters/Getty photo**

By the end of November, 2012, multiple news organizations have reported that Luo's house has been demolished. The Luo's purportedly came to amicable terms with local authorities. The agreed-upon sum was not disclosed under conditions of the agreement.[xv]

Luo's "House in the Middle of the Highway" image was without a doubt one of the most memorable modern Chinese illustrations of David vs. Goliath, second only to the Tank Man who single-handedly stopped the parade of a column of tanks in 1989. It should be noted that he pulled it off thanks to a host of factors, including collective resentment toward the forcible mass relocation necessitated by China's gargantuan infrastructure upgrade and engineering stunts such as the Three Gorges Dam and the massive Northbound Water Diversion program. Many have paid dearly in their own protest against the government's land seizure and forced eviction, with their own lives at times. According to the Human Right Watch's 2012 China Report, some 250-500 mass protests occur daily in China,[xvi] many of which are against the same abuse Luo valiantly fought. Their travails have been detailed in an Amnesty International Report entitled *"Standing Their Ground – Thousands Face Violent Eviction in China."*[xvii] In one of the 40 cases examined in the report, the municipal authority of Wenchang City, Sichuan Province, held a 20-month old baby as hostage until his mother signed the eviction order.

According to a *Daily Telegraph* report, some 40 Chinese resorted to self-immolation to protest against forced eviction in Sichuan Province.[xviii]

Disparity vs. Equalizer

On Jan 21, 2013, China's National Bureau of Statistics (NBS) released its first ever Gini coefficient for the past decade. The Gini coefficient measures the inequality among values of a frequency distribution (for example levels of income). A Gini coefficient of zero expresses perfect equality, where all values are the same (for example, where everyone has an exactly equal income). A Gini coefficient of one (100 on the percentile scale) expresses maximal inequality among values (for example where only one person has all the income).

The NBS-released Gini coefficient reached 0.474 in China in 2012, higher than the warning level of 0.40 set by the United Nations (The World Bank uses a Gini value greater than 0.40 as a predictor of future social unrest). The NBS claims that China's Gini coefficient, known colloquially in China as the rich-poor index, has retreated gradually since hitting a peak of 0.491 in 2008, dropping to 0.49 in 2009, 0.481 in 2010 and 0.477 in 2011. The index stood at 0.479 in 2003, 0.473 in 2004, 0.485 in 2005, 0.487 in 2006 and 0.484 in 2007.

These numbers are actually slightly higher than estimates put out by the United Nations (UN), the World Bank, the US Central Intelligence Agency (CIA), and the Organization for Economic Co-operation and Development (OECD). [xix] Based on the CIA's estimate, China's Gini index was at 0.47 for 2007 and ranks number 36 in the countries with highest Gini index. If we replace CIA's 0.47 with China's own official 0.484 (48.4%), China's ranking jumps to number 29, ahead of U.S. (No. 44), Japan (No. 74), India (No. 79) and all European countries except Switzerland.

The author feels obliged, though, to point out that China's NBS does not score high on credibility. The general lack of confidence in

NBS's numbers outside China has given birth to China Beige Book™, a quarterly report based on American-led private survey data collected in China.[xx] Even inside China, academic institutions sometimes contradict NBS's data. China's Gini coefficient for 2010, for example, was reported to be at 0.61 in Sept. 2012 by the Chinese Household Finance Survey Center of Southwestern University of Finance and Economics,[xxi] which is almost 12 percentage points higher than NBS's data released in 2013. No wonder NBS is often the butt of the joke in China. One of the well-known ones asks: If a Chinese marathon runner and a NBS bureaucrat get strangled in a desert together, who do you think will make out OK? The correct choice is the NBS bureaucrat, because he knows how to secretly "pack" water (or to adulterate things with water, if you catch the drift.)

It is fair to say that China has completely abandoned Mao's egalitarian legacy. The honorable nickname "the New Socialist China" has all but become a bitter joke. Chinese intellectuals, when commenting on the society's inequality, often quote the immortal verse of Tang Dynasty's great poet, Du Fu: "Leftovers in mansions stink high heaven, while the beggars freeze to death on the streets." ("朱门酒肉臭，路有冻死骨。")

While China could afford to spend a whopping $40 billion on the 2008 Summer Olympics and $300 million on the opening ceremony alone, its hospitals routinely deny treatment to those who are too poor to hand over the required down payment. While a coal mine tycoon in Shanxi Province spent a whopping ¥140 million ($22.5 million) on his daughter's wedding and dowry, a staggering 172 million Chinese (roughly 13% of the total population) live on less than $1.25 a day.[xxii]

Nowadays, $1.25 in China does not go very far. According to the *Starbuck Latte Index* published on Feb 23, 2013 in *Wall Street*

Journal, a Grande Latte costs $4.81 in Beijing, higher than in the Big Apple. The author himself has been to many of China's 390-plus Starbucks and can attest that the price is ridiculously steep. Though it is safe to assume that the 172 million Chinese living on less than $1.25 a day never visit a Starbucks, it is doubtful that anyone can buy enough food and shelter with a measly $1.25 in any part of China.

Updown Court, in Surrey, the UK's most opulent house, was sold for £35 million to an unidentified Chinese buyer in Oct, 2011. Photo Source: Wikipedia, under Creative Commons

The Telegraph

China shocked by death of five boys who lived in a bin

The deaths of five street children who poisoned themselves after lighting a fire to fend off the cold have triggered an outpouring of online grief and reinforced a national debate over China's growing wealth gap.

The five street children who died from carbon monoxide poisoning after starting charcoal fire inside bin, Bijie, Guizhou Province, China Photo: Rex Features

By Tom Phillips, Shanghai
1:13PM GMT 21 Nov 2012

 Print this article

A screenshot of *the Telegraph* report on the shocking death of five homeless children on Nov 21, 2012

It is hard to imagine that today's materialist, money-worshipping China used to be an egalitarian commune, whose supreme leader, Chairman Mao, abhorred money and was loath to touch it. It was rumored that he once opened an envelope sent by his secretary thinking it contained some documents. When he took out the contents, he was livid. The secretary had sent him some of his newly-disbursed book royalty money. Under Mao, prosperity for individuals was sacrificed for the sake of equality for the masses. Wealth had a bad reputation and was synonymous to inequality. This dogma was finally broken and abandoned when Mao's successor Deng Xiaoping boldly called for economic reform by allowing a "small group of people to prosper ahead of others."

Deng's broad-stroke blueprint for China's economic reform did not spell out the details on what would happen after this small group of Chinese had prospered to become the society's privileged elites. Little action has been seen from the Party's top leadership to address the devastating wealth gap, other than the usual empty words and a few poignant Kodak moments. The just-retired Chinese Premier, Wen Jabao, was shown on camera sharing a humble bowl of dumplings with a peasant family. An official news clip showed the newly-minted Communist Party General Secretary, Xi Jinping, holding hands with a village elderly.

So, other than death, is there any equalizer in the Chinese society? The answer is a resounding "Yes" according to Mr. Jack Ma, the founder of Alibaba.com. Mr. Ma is the Chinese version of Craig Newmark, the founder and principal owner of CraigsList.org, who strongly believed in the Web as the democratic community for the masses.

Bad air – that's right – is the greatest equalizer for all in China, says Mr. Ma. The privileged can have their expensive packaged water. They can have their imported medicines. But they have to breathe in the same choking, acrid air as we do, Mr. Ma points out in a public address, delivered in the wake of the worst-ever streak of smog in Beijing and other major cities in China.

In the two to three weeks leading to the Chinese New Year on Feb 10, 2013, Beijing's PM2.5 score – particles with diameters between 2.5 and 10 micrometers, a.k.a. coarse particles – reached the insane neighborhood of 800-900. The UN safety standard for PM2.5 is set at 25, while PM2.5 scores in major U.S. cities hover in the 30 – 60 range. The EPA maximum PM2.5 for any location in U.S. is set at 65.

Mr. Ma certainly made a great point. If death is the greatest equalizer and can be still be easily acquired by way of heavily polluted air, a vengeful justice has indeed been delivered by way of bad air in a bitterly divided China. "We are all going to suffer from three main types of cancers from now." Ma told his audience, "Liver cancer caused by the toxic water we drink; stomach cancer by the toxic food we eat; lung cancer by the polluted air we cannot escape from."

The Great Firewall of China vs. 27 Million Wall-climbers

The late Supreme Leader of China, Mr. Deng Xiaoping, is remembered for his candid and colorful speech. In an apparent allusion to freedom and democracy, Deng said, "Open the windows, breathe the fresh air and at the same time fight the flies and insects."

His words proved to be seminal. Unlike North Korea, which still bans the Internet, China embraced it in 1994. The Internet in China in those early days was no more than a skeletal fishnet featuring dial-up connections. Still, the Chinese government got extremely uneasy with the "flies and insects" that wandered into China through this opened window. By 1998, when state-owned ISP's started selling broadband connections, it took firm action to build a screen to filter the traffic through this window.

Enter the Golden Shield, an $800 million project, commonly known as the Great Firewall or GFW, to be operated by the Ministry of Public Security. Since its inception in 1998, the Great Firewall went from using brute IP blocking to implementing cutting edge technologies such as DNS filtering and redirection, URL filtering, packet filtering, man-in-the-middle attack and connection reset, network enumeration, speech and face recognition. Today, it is speculated that some 60,000 people work for the Great Firewall of China.

The GFW's tight grip on Chinese surfers is devastating. First of all, the stalwarts of the Internet, namely, Google, Facebook, Twitter and YouTube, are blatantly blocked. And the Chinese government's blacklist is whimsical and largely retaliatory. After the *New York Times* ran a lengthy report on October 25, 2012 revealing the $2.7 billion of hidden wealth held by the family of then-Premier Mr. Wen Jiabao, nytimes.com has been blocked in China.

Secondly, the GFW is effective mainly thanks to its terrifying Panopticon effect. With the largest number of imprisoned journalists and cyberdissidents in the world, China puts the burden of enforcing its ubiquitous Internet censorship on all stakeholders of the Web, from search engines, online markets, and social media communities to individual surfers.

Just how bad is China's online censorship? The author ran a quick test with China's largest and most popular search engine Baidu.com by searching for the world's only imprisoned Nobel Laureate, the 2010 Nobel Peace Prize winner, Mr. Liu Xiaobo. The term used in the search was "刘晓波 08 宪章" ("Liu Xiaobo, '08 Charter"), Liu's political manifesto, and Baidu returned only one result.

A search on Liu Xiaobo and his '08 Charter generated only one result on Baidu.com.

The sole link delivered by Baidu against my search opens to a statement of criticism and disapproval from a spokesperson regarding Liu's winning the Nobel Peace Prize. Not surprisingly, the author ran the same search in Google and got about 163,000 returns.

Like the brick and mortar Great Wall of China, the Great Firewall of China may prove to be yet ineffective in the long run. Zigzagging from Shanhaiguan on the Bohai Gulf in the east to Jiayuguan on the edge of Tarim Basin in the west, through the tough northern terrains, China's iconic Great Wall boasts a massive length of more than 6,000 kilometers. An ancient civil engineering feat notwithstanding, the Great Wall did little to defend China against nomadic Mongols in the 13th century and the Manchu's in the 17th century.

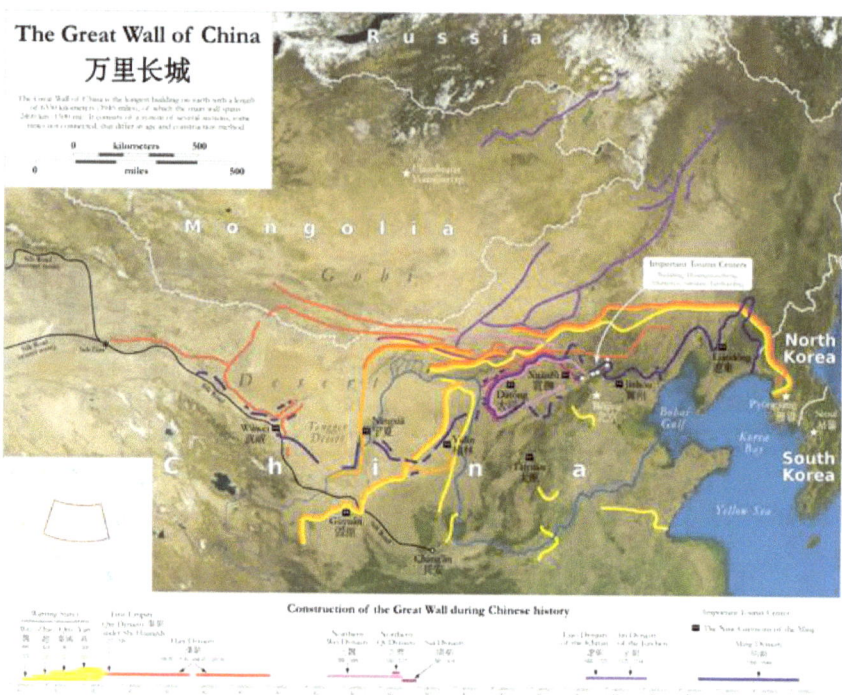

The Great Wall of China. Photo Courtesy of Wikipedia, under Creative Commons.

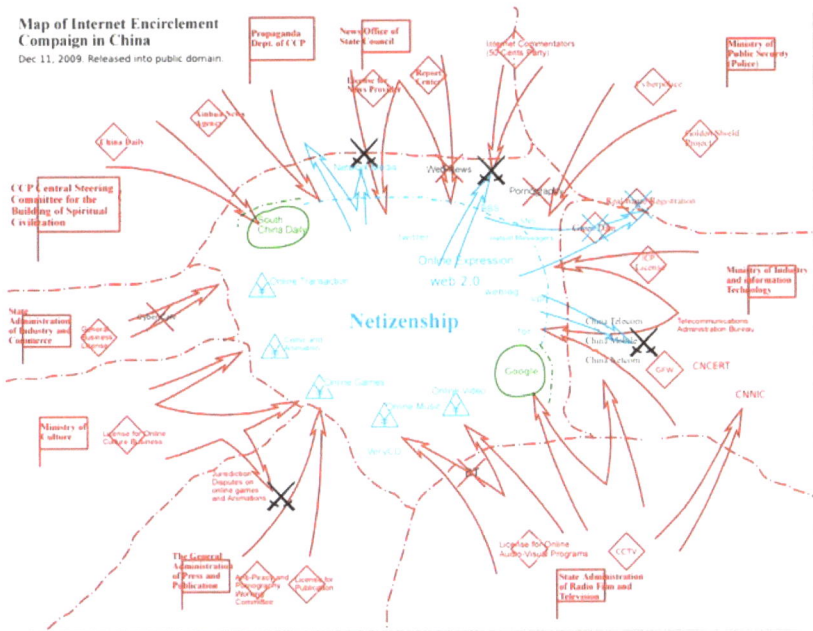

A diagram compiled by Harvard's Berkman Center for Internet and Society in 2009, demonstrating the GFW's massive choke on China's Internet. Source: Public domain.

Today, the Great Firewall of China is suffering more or less the same ineffectual fate as its brick and mortar sibling: An estimated 27 million Chinese surfers routinely circumvent the Great Firewall, by performing cyber acrobatics, known in China as "climbing the wall."

According to statistics released by *The Epoch Times*, China's brave army of wall-climbers consists mainly of male college students located in Beijing, China's eastern seaboard and southern coastal regions. Three quarters of the wall-climbers, most of them between the ages of 19 and 28, are college graduates.[xxiii]

For now, wall-climbing is not for the vast majority of China's 538,000,000 Internet users,[xxiv] as all wall-climbing tools present a learning curve and the clear and present danger of getting caught. The tools the Chinese wall-climbers use range from good old Web proxies for the casual, occasional wall-climbers, to corporate VPN,

SSH tunneling, and installed applications on computers and devices for the die-hard, everyday ones.

Thanks to these 27 million brave souls, the Great Firewall of China has failed to isolate China. Whatever you post online outside China, if it happens to be apropos of China, rest assured that your voice is heard on the other side of the Great Firewall as well.

A Chinese wall-climber reposted the news on Change.org about Archbishop Desmond Tutu's petition to Chinese Communist Chief Xi Jinping, signed by more than 427,000 people as of this writing. This is a screenshot, of which the url is concealed to protect the source.

First Time Ever vs. Just another One of Those

As expected, Chinese Communist Party Chief Xi Jinping was appointed as the new President of China on March 14, 2013 by the *National People's Congress*, China's rubberstamp parliament. However, the perfunctory voting of general assembly preceding the appointment threw a curveball: Out of the 2,963 valid ballots, seven went missing, three abstained, one opposed.

This one solitary opposition is the very first ever in Communist China's history of a top leader's appointment. China's state media pretended that it never happened, or that it was nothing of any significance. But of course, it caused quite a stir on the Chinese social networks and caught the attention of the foreign media.

Moment of truth: A live tally monitor at the National People's Congress shows 2,952 member voted Aye, one voted Nay and three abstained on the appointment of Party Chief Xi Jinping as the President of China. Photo source: widely circulated online in China. Origin unclear.

Who was the *enfant terrible* who voted no? The question caused a frenzy of speculation on the Chinese web.

On the same day, Mr. Zhang Dejiang, the 3rd-ranked member of the Chinese Communist Party's Politburo Standing Committee, was appointed as the Chairman of the National People's Congress Standing Committee while five other preordained career bureaucrats, Messrs. Wang Shengjun, Zhang Ping, Chen Zhu, Wan Exiang and Wang Chen were appointed as Vice Chairmen of the National People's Congress Standing Committee, after similar perfunctory votes.

Four days later, Mr. Wang Cheng, an attorney in Hangzhou, filed a lawsuit with the Supreme People's Court of the People's Republic of China, alleging afore-mentioned appointments unconstitutional. The ground for his allegation? It turns out that Chinese Constitution has a stipulation explicitly prohibits any incumbent member of the government's executive or judiciary branches from taking a seat in the National People's Congress Standing Committee, namely, the legislative branch.

Mr. Wang Cheng's was a first-ever lawsuit against China's parliament and it appears that he did his homework: The Chinese Constitution does have such a stipulation and the six individuals whose appointments were in question were indeed incumbent top-ranking members of the central government's executive and judiciary branches. The following is a list of their then-incumbent positions:

Zhang Dejiang: Vice-Premier in charge of energy, telecommunications, and transportation.

Wang Shengjun: President of the Supreme People's Court of the People's Republic of China

Zhang Ping: Chairman of the National Development and Reform Commission, a prominent department within the State Council of the People's Republic of China.

Chen Zhu: Minister of Health of P.R.China.

Wan Exiang: Vice President of the Supreme People's Court of China.

Wang Chen: Director of the Information Office of the State Council.

It deserves a clarification that these gentlemen did resign from their then-incumbent executive or judiciary branch positions; however, the resignations all happened after their appointments into the National People's Congress Standing Committee. This clear violation of the Constitution was more of a careless error than deliberate abuse. But it goes to show how little attention the National People's Congress has or is paying to the country's Constitution. After all, nobody has ever taken it seriously. That is, nobody until Mr. Wang Cheng.

According to the well-established procedures of China's Supreme Court, it has to deliver a decision on whether to hear a case or not within seven days of its filing. Mr. Wang Cheng mailed his filing to the Court on March 18 by Express Mail Service and got the delivery confirmation on March 19. Seven days quickly went by after that and Mr. Wang has not heard a thing from the Court. In the meantime, Mr. Wang's two major weibo (microblog) accounts got mysteriously deleted. Other than a few Chinese social networks, Mr. Wang also got largely snubbed by mainstream Chinese media. As of the publication of this book, Mr. Wang's suit is still a developing story.

Mr. Wang Cheng, Esq. in an undated photo posted on his law firm's website.

These days, China floods the world with fascinating headlines every day. If you look carefully, most of the headline-makers are first-ever incidents: 13,000 dead pigs clogging Shanghai's Whampoa (Huangpu) River; six dead out of a total of 16 confirmed N7H9 Avian Flu cases as of April 5, 2013 and, etc. Last month, China's first lady, Mme. Peng Liyuan dazzled the world when she accompanied her husband, China's newly minted President Xi Jinping, on a state visit to Tanzania. She emerged from the airplane cabin wearing high-heel shoes that exposed her elegant toes.

China's glamorous first lady Madame Peng Liyuan sporting open toe high heels at Tanzania's Dar Es Salaam International Airport.

But like many "first ever" things that have come to pass in China, the knee-jerk reaction to these headlines will fizzle out soon. The first time a Chinese national married a foreigner may have wreaked havoc in China's national psyche. But today, a Chinese marrying a foreigner is just one of those things. According to the statistics released by China's Civil Affairs Bureau in 2005, the previous decade (from 1995 through 2004) saw more than 600,000 registered international marriages.

Similarly, gay and lesbians in China – not LGBT, as bisexuals and transgenders have not quite gained recognition yet – don't make headlines in China nowadays, except when they stage an "awareness" demonstration that involves flashy attire or paint-on bras. They are just members of the Chinese masses. In fact, their existence is so well tolerated and taken for granted that they've earned a new euphemism: Comrades. The yesteryear's Communist exclusive salutation is now used in casual circumstances to refer to gays or lesbians: a lesbian is just a "female comrade" (女同志) while a gay man is simply a "male comrade" (男同志).

The Chinese are smart enough to understand that one shocking headline and what Andy Warhol defined as "15-minute fame" doesn't bring much material change to their country. After all, the great philosopher-dictator Chairman Mao explained the rule of change better than *I Ching*, when he said, "Quantitative changes amount to a qualitative change."

Yes will this one solitary opposition vote usher in a new era in the *National People's Congress*, and China's politics in general? Will we see more opposition to the pre-ordaining of a government office? So much that the opposition votes out-numbers the supporters? Well, never say never. Way too many "first ever" things have happened in China, and are now dismissed as "one of those" things when a copycat occurs. Acknowledgement of difference may be just the baby step the world's largest populace is currently taking toward a democratic future.

Same Old Drama vs. Much More Critical Audience

According to columnist Peggy Noonan, Margaret Thatcher said once to her aides: "I don't need to be told *what*, I need to be told *how*." Meaning I have a vision, you have to tell me how we can implement it. Ms. Noonan went on to offer her observation, "Politics now, in England as well as America, is dominated by politicians who are technicians. They always know how to do it. They just don't know what to do."[xxv]

Ms. Noonan's observation will be right on the nose if it is applied to today's China. Ever since the passing of Deng Xiaoping in 1997, China has been ruled by a new class of Communist technocrats, who are extremely good at execution, but fairly clueless as to the next level they plan to take China to.

These technocrats usually have an engineering degree or background, and have climbed the Communist leadership ladder after the death of Mao Zedong in 1976. They have never fought in a war. They have never been in any position of influence or importance when Communist China underwent its most tumultuous metamorphosis – the Civil War, the Korean War, the Great Leap Forward and the Cultural Revolution. The last known crisis that has seriously threatened the rule of the Communist party was the 1989 Tiananmen Square Student Movement, but that was deftly handled by Deng Xiaoping.

Deng Xiaoping, the last great helmsman of the Chinese Communist Party, hand-picked his successor Jiang Zemin, and his successor-to-successor, Hu Jintao. In a sense, Deng had set the China Boat on a pre-chartered route for decade and half after his death, until late 2012 when Mr. Xi Jinping was selected as the Party Chief for the next 10 years.

It is a fair to say that the China Boat is officially sailing on unchartered water now under Xi Jinping's untested reign. Unlike his two predecessors who had the opportunity to consult a dying gerontocracy, the first-generation Communist revolutionaries are completely gone now. Now and then, Mr. Xi encounters tricky situations whereby he cannot take a page out of Mao or Deng's playbook to deal with. That's also when we see him fumble.

One prime example is the long-awaited trial of Bo Xilai, a flamboyant and rambunctious leftist who was ousted last year to clear the path for party leadership transition. Bo was the charismatic and demagogic mayor of Chongqing, China's largest nationally governed municipality and was a serious contender for seat in the Communist Party's Politburo Standing Committee before his ouster. While his wife Gu Kailai and his one-time comrade-in-arms and lieutenant Wang Lijun were both put through criminal trial and sentenced to jail, Bo has remained under house arrest since March 2012, creating a controversial legal impasse for the Communist leadership who constantly proclaims that all matters in the People's Republic must undergo due legal process, but never offer any explanation on the fate of Bo.

On China's social network sites, rumors about Bo abounds. If these rumors have any credibility, Bo may just be the tough nut to crack. Throughout the Communist Party's history, a disgraced leader is supposed to show remorse, in exchange for leniency. Bo, never a conformist, apparently does not want to play along. Once widely spread version of the rumors is that he is staging a "no-shaving" strike and has since grown an insanely large and bushy beard. That, plus predictably his defiant behavior in the courtroom, will definitely not play well on national TV, should Xi decides to put Bo through a criminal trial.

So, like a typical clueless man dealing with a predicament, Xi is procrastinating, while Bo remains a spectacle on the national theater.

And judging from the wisecracks and rumors floating on China's social networks, the drama on Bo's fate is far from being forgotten. Instead, how Bo is going to be tried remains to be a litmus test for China's legal system. After all, the majority of Chinese still view China's legal system as a dramatic theater where they get a great deal of entertainment from. Given the pent-up interest and long suspense on the Bo Xilai case, it is shaping up like a really good one.

In a very recent rude awakening, the Chinese Communist Party learned just how unsympathetic the theater audience has become. On April 15, 2013, "People's Forum", an online forum managed by the Party's mouthpiece People's Daily, put out a multiple choice survey on question about "Confidence, beliefs and ideology." But they made a serious mistake by providing "I don't agree" answer as one of the choices. The survey result was so embarrassingly bad that the survey was promptly pulled down and its result wiped out, but not before some netizens captured some damaging screenshots.

The survey result is translated as follows:

1. Do you agree that the Chinese Communist Party has enough courgage and wisdom to push forward the Reform?

	Votes	Percentage
i) I Agree Completely	170	7.41%
ii) I Agree	135	5.88%
iii) I am Not Sure	304	13.25%
iv) I Disagree	1685	73.45%

2. Do you agree with the assertion that "Adhere to and develop Socialism with Chinese Characteristics is in the fundamental interest of the vast majority of the people?"

	Votes	Percentage
i) I Agree Completely	120	5.25%
ii) I Agree	103	4.51%
iii) I am Not Sure	207	9.06%
iv) I Disagree	1856	81.19%

3. Do you agree with the assertion that "Only the Chinese Communist Party is capable of leading us on the journey to develop Socialism with Chinese Characteristics?"

	Votes	Percentage
i) I Agree Completely	110	4.80%
ii) I Agree	96	4.18%
iii) I am Not Sure	194	8.46%
iv) I Disagree	1894	82.56%

4. What do you think of the "One party rules while multiple parties participate" system?

	Votes	Percentage
i) I Agree Completely	159	6.93%

ii) I Agree	124	5.41%
iii) I am Not Sure	177	7.72%
iv) I Disagree	1833	79.94%

滚动新闻 ▶ 新加坡还要当多久 "李家坡" 最杰：良渚古城改造设防坡毁江古城

:: 问卷调查

"信心·信念·信仰" 调查

习主席的 "中国梦" 承载了亿万人民的梦想和重托，重塑了中华民族伟大复兴的希望。实现中国梦，需要坚定的信心，执着的信念，和崇高的信仰。惟有自信的信心和坚定不移的信念，使我们更加更坚地在中国特色社会主义信仰的旗帜下，凝聚团结，万众一心，为实现共同理想而奋斗。当亿万人民的信心、信念、信仰汇聚为共同坚守，我们才能用13亿人的智慧和力量汇聚起不可战胜的磅礴力量，共同实现梦想。欢迎参与人民论坛网问卷调查中心 "信心·信念·信仰" 调查。

1、您是否赞同中国共产党有足够的勇气和智慧加快推进改革？

A、完全赞同	票数：170	7.41%
B、赞同	票数：135	5.88%
C、不清楚	票数：304	13.25%
D、不赞同	票数：1685	73.45%

2、您赞同 "坚持和发展中国特色社会主义有利于最广大人民的根本利益" 的说法么？

A、完全赞同	票数：120	5.50%
B、赞同	票数：103	4.49%
C、不知道	票数：207	9.02%
D、不赞同	票数：1856	80.91%

3、您赞同 "只有中国共产党才能带领人民走好中国特色社会主义道路" 的说法么？

A、完全赞同	票数：110	4.80%
B、赞同	票数：96	4.10%
C、不知道	票数：194	8.45%
D、不赞同	票数：1894	82.56%

4、您对中国 "一党执政、多党参政" 的制度怎么看？

A、完全赞同	票数：159	6.93%
B、赞同	票数：124	5.41%
C、不知道	票数：177	7.72%
D、不赞同	票数：1833	79.94%

A People's Daily Snafu: **A short-lived "People's Forum" survey showed thousands of polled choose to categorically disagree with the Communist Party. More than 70% disagree on all questions.**

Bullshit Talks while Money Walks

Warren Buffet, the legendary investment guru, offered a famous observation when commenting on the academic community's pathological aversion to his investment approach, "Well, it may be all right in practice, but it will never work in theory." When poking fun, Wall Street investment bankers and traders often paraphrase Buffet's words as: We know it works in practice, but will it work in theory?

Nowadays, when the ruling elites of the Chinese Communist Party ask themselves that question, they are not poking fun; they are dead serious. On one hand, they know that the market economy they have borrowed from the West works and has brought about wonders; on the other hand they are not so stupid as to borrow the other goodies in the same Western package, such as a multi-party democratic social system.

To sustain their dictatorial rule of the Chinese nation, they must feign their faith in the communist doctrine, since one of Karl Marx's main social prescription is the "democratic dictatorship of the proletarians." (Mao's interpretation.) However, anyone with half a brain knows that the migrant workers – the one social class that best fits Karl Marx's categorization of the proletarians – are social pariahs in today's China. It is about the biggest insult one can place on them to say that the communist dictatorship represents their interest.

Similar to what transpired in Hans Christian Andersen's tale of "The Emperor's New Clothes", the rulers and the ruled in China both know that the Communist Party's claim to their communist or socialist faith is as bogus as the emperor's new clothes. Today's China presents a classic snapshot of the crass and brutal capitalist society the Chinese Communist Party used to scare people with, with vivid details flushed out with "Chinese-style" ("the ugly Chinese," see Cyber Slang vs. *People's Daily*) extremeness. Karl Marx and Vladimir Lenin must have turned in their graves when they heard a communist state like China routinely imprisons its labor activists. In Labor Rights Now President Don Stillman's words, "China deserves a gold medal for labor repression."

Chinese labor activists holding a candlelight vigil on June 13, 2012 for Li Wangyang, a fellow activist who served 21 years in prison and died soon after his release. Photo source: Wikimedia/public domain

Naturally, until some Karl Rove-type consigliere comes up with a brilliant theory proving that the Chinese society has some semblance to a communist or socialist blueprint, the mandarins in Beijing just have to keep on pretending that the emperor's new clothes are on their butt-naked body. A classic case of "bullshit talks" will just have to go on.

Bullshit Talks: members of the National People's Congress (China's rubberstamp parliament) snoozing away while the big potatoes read through their marathon reports. This is a screenshot collage taken from club.china.com, where user-contributed photos were compiled in a report at http://club.china.com/data/thread/1011/2755/88/37/5_1.html

However, in a country where the citizens cannot vote with ballots, they vote with their feet. The poor and have-nots leave their backwater home regions for the industrial heartlands and coastal areas, to become migrant workers; the super rich and haves also vote with their feet: they emigrate to the West.

Under a law passed by the Congress in 1990, the U.S. grants up to 10,000 green cards annually to alien investors who have invested at least $1,000,000 in the U.S. (the minimum investment amount is lowered to $500,000 if the investment is toward a designated high unemployment rate or rural area.) According to the statistics released by U.S. Citizenship and Immigration Services (USCIS) for 2012, China tops all the rest of the world combined with a whopping 5,923 investment immigrants to the U.S., accounting for more than 80% of the green cards issued to alien investors.

In June 2012, a Chinese traveler entering Canada via Vancouver International Airport was caught carrying a suitcase full of undeclared cash in the record amount of $177,495.50. From April 2011 to June 2012, over $15 million of unreported funds was intercepted at this airport, Canada's second busiest. Almost two-thirds, or $9.7 million, arrived from China, according to a *Vancouver Sun* report.[xxvi] According to a survey released by The Boston Consulting Group and Private Bank Division of China Construction Bank in December, 2011, offshore wealth held by Chinese high net worth (HNW) individuals increased to $7.8 trillion, up from $7.5 trillion in 2009. The report also asserts that "...unlike their counterparts in US and Europe, most HNW individuals in China are less concerned about taxes and more concerned about safety and stability."[xxvii]

If China's ruling elites enjoy "bullshit talks," they definitely get nervous watching "money walks." Mr. Wang Qishan, the sixth ranking member of the Standing Committee of the Politburo of the Chinese Communist Party, issued a grave warning to the elites of the Party in late 2012 when he forcibly suggested that they read de Tocqueville's *The Old Regime and the Revolution*. The gist of de Tocqueville's masterpiece is inevitably subject to eternal debate, but in the ruling circle of China, it is more or less interpreted as: When the subjects are mired in the harsh tyranny of a ruler, they somehow tend to behave; but when the ruler voluntarily reforms the government and improves the subjects' quality of life, they are more inclined to overthrow the ruler by launching a revolution. So, watch out, Chinese Communist Party, now that your subjects have had a taste of a better material life.

Obviously, the mandarins in Beijing have begun to see the writing on the wall, as evidenced by the warning delivered by the newly minted Party Chief Xi Jinping repeatedly, in which he asserts that the Chinese Communist Party would collapse, if it could not seek the opportunity to reform and improve governance. If the suffering of China's extremely poor is routinely ignored by the ruling elites, it is to contrary when it comes to signals sent by the extremely rich. There is solid evidence that they have taken notice of the expedited fleeing of the wealthy, and the flight of wealth, as a result.

In one subtle move to combat flight of wealth, China announced that a new law taking effect this summer will grant foreign permanent residence card holders the same rights as a Chinese citizen and, at the same time, massively increase the number of such cards issued annually. This is not a mere gesture to reduce the hassles the 600,000 expatriates living in China – many of them overseas Chinese – must endure to maintain their stay, it is also an enticement to lure those who have fled to return. After all, nothing can be strictly taken for the face value. A Chinese green card is basically an immunity card to the super rich who have already bought their foreign identity. It basically says: OK, you are no longer subject to the totalitarian rule of China, but please keep your business in China. Let's at least keep the money end of equation a win-win situation.

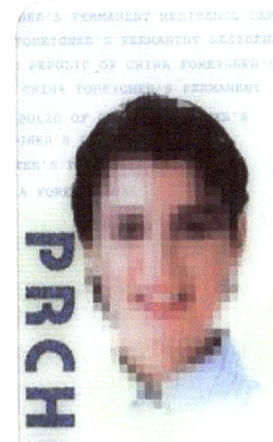

XXX110074110419

姓名 /Name

SAMPLE,
PERMANENT RESIDENCE CARD

性别/Sex　出生日期 /Date of birth

女/F　　**1974.11.04**

国籍/ Nationality

样本/XXX

证件有效期/Valid for

2004.09.30-2014.09.29

中 华 人 民 共 和 国 公 安 部
Ministry of Public Security of the People's Republic of China

A sample Permanent Residence Card issued by Ministry of Public Security. Source: Wikimedia.

Epilogue, or a List of Spoilers for the Dinner Party

It is risky to make an assertion about the fate of China; she has repeatedly proved many people, scholars and politicians alike, wrong. In his famed book *My Country and My People*, the late Dr. Lin Yutang charted China's cyclical history and discovered that she is conquered, and subsequently rejuvenated, by an alien nation about every 300 years, and that she always manages to assimilate the invaders into her grand culture. Well, that prediction did not quite pan out, as China has not been conquered by a foreign power since the Manchu invasion in the 17th century. For some two hundred years after Napoleon Bonaparte delivered his foresight on China – "Let China sleep, for when she wakes, she will shake the world" – China had remained largely asleep, until recently, when she became the world's second largest economy and gave the impression that she could shake the world.

Perhaps, when enough time elapses, a safe prediction on China is bound to ring true. When asked what impact the 1789 French Revolution had had on the world's history, the late Premier Zhou Enlai of China was rumored to have answered, "It's too early to tell." True, when he answered that question in the early 1970's, the French revolution was not even 200 years old.

But the world community is not going to give China another 200 years to ponder her social future. The world needs to see the most populous nation at peace, to see its citizens' rights and dignity respected. It is not a comforting sight to see the world's largest populace living under an abusive one-party dictatorship, for evil knows no borders; what a dictatorship does to its own people, it can also do to its neighbors – at least its weak neighbors.

The author's assertion that the next revolutions in China are going to be dinner parties, like all predictions, can be rendered invalid under some contingent circumstances. The following are two of the *force majeure* that may throw China into a turmoil and prove yet again that Mao was correct in asserting that revolution is NOT a dinner party.

A war with Japan. Diplomatically, it is now a challenging time for the Chinese government, as China's territorial disputes with Japan and its South China Sea neighbors are escalating. Internally, the Chinese people are quite pissed at the lack of clarity their government has demonstrated when dealing with neighborly disputes. They reminisce about the good old days when China exercised unequivocal foreign policies under Mao and Deng. China was a much poorer nation back then, but her voice was firm and decisive, and followed by even firmer actions, as demonstrated in the Korean War and Vietnam War, and China's brief wars with Vietnam in the late 1970's.

The willpower of the Chinese government is now being challenged by Japan, a nation that has proven to the world that they will always fight till the last man when it comes to the defense of what they believe is theirs.

At the center of China's territorial dispute with Japan is a group of uninhabited rocky islands in the East China Sea currently controlled by Japan, known in China and Taiwan as *Diaoyu Islands* and as *Senkaku Islands* in Japan. No matter how much pragmatic significance one strives to attach to the islands, it is hard to explain the amount of fervor each side devotes to this dispute. It is a confrontation building up daily like an eventual showdown of will and war power.

In this showdown, Japan sees a seriously threatening neighbor, who most likely will demand a yard if given an inch. Japan's worry is not groundless. As some Chinese historians claim, Okinawa was once Chinese, or at least a Chinese suzerainty. So these rocky islands are just the beginning of more serious territory disputes to come. For Japan, defending the Senkaku Islands today is as important as defending Iwo Jima in the Pacific War.

In the same showdown, China sees Japan's imperialist arrogance as a ruthless aggressor who does not even feign remorse for its atrocious war crimes against the Chinese. Adding insult to injury, Japan has never treated China as a winner of that war, though China was an Allied Cosigner on Japan's unconditional surrender. After all, China was to some extend the beneficiary of charity: The Soviet Red Army drove the Japanese out of Manchuria while the Americans completely routed Japan's Imperial Navy in the Pacific; not to mention the devastation of A-bombs dropped on Hiroshima and Nagasaki.

The Chinese are smart enough to realize that the Japanese only respect people who have defeated them and that the Chinese do not count as one. After all, Japan has never lost a major war with China in the past, not even to Kublai Khan's China. When the massive fleet commanded by the Mongol Emperor of China was poised to conquer Japan in 1725, an even more massive typhoon brought about the complete demise of the fleet. The Japanese were so grateful to the typhoon they have since referred to it as kamikaze. (Japanese: 神風, devine wind.)

As such, both sides know that there is a lot riding on a territorial dispute over the group of rocky islands. If any military conflict actually erupts, large or small, it would feel like an all-in gamble for both sides. There is just no graceful way for either side to back down. As a result, despite the heated rhetoric, neither the Chinese nor the Japanese wants to start a war unless they absolutely have to.

The Chinese simply have their hands tied. They have way too many household matters to sort out, the least among which is to quietly modernize its navy. For heaven's sake, what does the Chinese navy have to boast? The one aircraft carrier they bought from a Ukraine scrap yard? Japan had 31 carriers in WWII. Today, the U.S. and Japan Mutual Defense Assistance Agreement basically stipulates that a war with Japan equals to a war with the U.S., whose military superiority in the Pacific is undeniable.

Politically, it is wise and convenient for both the Chinese and the Japanese governments to engage in a cold war. That way they can continue to satisfy the furious nationalism on either side with carefully crafted and unrelenting rhetoric.

Disputed islands. Source: Wikimedia Commons

However, under one extreme circumstance, the Chinese government will not hesitate to go into war with Japan over the disputed group of islands. That is when there occurs a massive unrest inside China, something with a magnitude akin to that of the mass protest preceding the 1989 Tainanmen Square Massacre. In a memorandum to President Obama, Cheng Li, Director of Research at John L. Thornton China Center, claims that China's official data reveal that there are roughly 180,000 mass protests annually, or about 500 incidents per day.[xxviii] Any one of these mass protests has the potential of escalating into a serious threat to the Chinese Communist Party's one-party rule.

To get out of trouble when their legitimacy is under serious challenge, the mandarins in Beijing cannot resort to a bloody crackdown as they did in 1989. That would be a sure recipe to start a massive Arab Spring style violent revolution in China and beget their obituary. Instead, they will immediately resort to a war with Japan as an emergency rescue. The war can be started as a response to a Japanese miscalculation, or via a deliberate Chinese provocation. The blood and smoke of a war against China's most hated enemy will immediately appeal to a nationalist fervor, and give the mandarins in Beijing the justification to put the nation under a military curfew, buying them time to systematically crack down any opposition in the name of the motherland.

Victory or defeat, the 1.3 billion Chinese will lose whatever little personal freedom they have acquired over the past three decades. They will realize that the dinner party is now over, that in terms of China's march toward democracy, a war with a neighbor sets the clock back by at least half a century.

Ethnic unrest. Democracy is a healthy social mechanism, a process that offers fair participation to the stakeholders of a society. But it is not a guarantee of equality. The U.S. has been a democracy since its birth, but it took its time to abolish slavery, and segregation for that matter. India is considered a democracy, but it still endorses a brutal caste system.

Would the ethnic minorities – the Mongols, Uigurs, Tibetans and etc. – be better off in a democratic China? Not necessarily. A democracy measures a stakeholder's importance by its relative weight, or simply, its population. Han Chinese accounts for about 92% of China's population. Their sheer number gives their voice the natural veto power to any minority's. It is pretty safe to say that China's ethnic minorities are not really motivated by the Han Chinese's general pursuit of a more democratic society. For them, the survival of their own culture and rights to their ancestral land bears a higher priority and they would not hesitate to defend their fundamental interests, even if doing so retards China's general progression to democracy.

Plus, a collateral damage of China's worsening wealth disparity is undoubtedly its minorities. These disgruntled groups have lost the cradle-to-coffin state welfare they used to get in the Mao era; at the same time, few of them have been privileged enough to hop on the get-rich-first bandwagon.

A Uighur shoe peddler at Lhasa's Parkhor Flee Market on Aug. 13, 2009. ©Chew Man.

Despite their small population, minority groups like Mongols, Uigurs and Tibetans occupy a vast land mass in China. As China industrializes itself to the teeth, the natural resources from these minority groups' ancestral lands become critical and indispensable. When explaining China's double digit GDP growth and dominance in manufacturing, Western scholars unanimously cite cheap labor costs. Nobody mentions the cheap energy China is getting from these minority groups' ancestral lands. But the minorities know that they are being shortchanged. And they express their anger in different ways: The Tibetans via self-immolation and the Uigurs via sharpened and brandishing machetes. The Mongols are mute, and for good reason: Today, Mongols only account for 19% of the total population inhabiting their ancestral land.

The Uigur and the Tibetan ancestral lands, namely China's Xinjiang Autonomous Region and Tibet Autonomous Region, are different. They are physically very challenging for the average Han Chinese to inhabit. Despite Communist China's unrelenting effort to systematically colonize them, many rural areas still remain as the Wild Wild West.

Peace in China's West takes much more effort than what meets the eye. A Han Communist cadre smiling with a Uigur cantaloupe vendor for the TV camera in a Xinjiang agora tells you that there are a dozen gendarmerie soldiers patrolling nearby. And every Wednesday at Lhasa's Parkhor Corner or in front of Jokhang Monastery, you can spot more plainclothes police milling around than Tibetan pilgrims.

Chinese gendarmerie soldiers patrolling Parkhor Street, Lhasa, on Aug. 12, 2009. ©Chew Man.

It is a high liability maintenance that could go wrong any day. And when a sizable ethnic unrest erupts, the mandarins in Beijing can use it as an excuse to put the country under military curfew, claiming that the unrest is a result of a larger scale foreign conspiracy. When that happens, the dinner party is also over and the democracy clock is turned back.

###

~~~

If you liked this book, please post your review on Amazon, or send it to me.

Hearty thanks – M. Eigh

Eigh.com@gmail.com

~~~

[i] Report on an Investigation of the Peasant Movement in Hunan" (March 1927), Selected Works, Vol. I, p. 28.

[ii] Problems of War and Strategy" (November 6, 1938), Selected Works, Vol. II, p. 224.

[iii] CIA's involvement in the 1973 Chilean coup has been widely speculated and all but admitted to in a telephone conversation that took place between Kissinger and Nixon five days after the coup. The Kissinger Telcons: Kissinger Telcons on Chile, National Security Archive Electronic Briefing Book No. 123, edited by Peter Kornbluh, posted May 26, 2004.

[iv] Whelan, James, *Out of the Ashes: The Life, Death and Transfiguration of Democracy in Chile*, 1989, pp. 511-512 and 519-520.

[v] Ezra Vogel's Deng Xiaoping biography hits Chinese bookstores, *China Daily*, Jan. 17, 2013

[vi] Based on composite data from China's Sixth National Census, dated Nov. 1, 2010, released on April 28, 2011 and the U.S. Census Bureau International Program's International Data Base.

[vii] Wikipedia, List of countries by GDP (nominal) per capita, based on 2011 figures.

[viii] *A beloved Chinese comic gets the silent treatment*, September 09, 2010, By Megan K. Stack, Los Angeles Times

[ix] *The True Story of Ah Q*, first published in the *Beijing Morning News* supplement as a serial in 1921 through 1922.

[x] *Li Gang incident*, October 16, 2010

[xi] *Did a Chinese Safety Official Just Get Caught Smiling at a Horrific Accident Scene?* August 27, 2012, by David Wertime, Tea Leaf Nation

[xii] Corruption in China, Wikipedia

[xiii] This famous quote, a well known aphorism in journalism, is attributed to Alfred Harmsworth, a British newspaper magnate (1865–1922), New York Sun editor John B. Bogart (1848–1921) and Charles Anderson Dana (1819–1897).

[xiv] *Lei Feng*, Wikipedia.

[xv] *China's "House in the Middle of the Highway" Has Been Demolished*, by Mike Opelka, Dec 1, 2012, *The Blaze*.

[xvi] *World Report 2012: China, Events of 2011*, third paragraph. Human Rights Watch.

[xvii] *Standing Their Ground – Thousands Face Violent Eviction in China*, Amnesty International.

[xviii] *Chinese setting themselves on fire to protest against forced evictions*, The Telegragh, Feb 03, 2013

[xix] List of countries by income equality, Wikipedia

[xx] China Beige Book (CBB) International

[xxi] *China's Gini Index at 0.61, University Report Says*, Caixin Online.

[xxii] Poverty in the People's Republic of China, Wikipedia

[xxiii] 大陸網民：中國翻牆網民狀況調查. The Epoch Times.

[xxiv] *Top 20 Countries with the Highest Number of Internet Users*, Internet World Stats, July, 2012.

[xxv] *Britain Remembers a Great Briton*, the Wall Street Journal, April 22, 2013.

[xxvi] *Vancouver airport tops country in seizures of undeclared cash*, The Vancouver Sun.

[xxvii] *China Wealth 2011*, The Boston Consulting Group

[xxviii] *China in Revolution and War*, Brookings.edu.